IMAGES
of England

BECKENHAM AND WEST WICKHAM

The main hall at Wickham Hall, when new in 1897. See also pp. 116-117.

IMAGES

of England

BECKENHAM AND WEST WICKHAM

Compiled by
Simon Finch

TEMPUS

First published 1999
Copyright © London Borough of Bromley, 1999

Tempus Publishing Limited
The Mill, Brimscombe Port,
Stroud, Gloucestershire, GL5 2QG

ISBN 0 7524 1518 2

Typesetting and origination by
Tempus Publishing Limited
Printed in Great Britain by
Midway Clark Printing, Wiltshire

The Rising Sun and cottages, Upper Elmers End Road, Beckenham, c. 1900.

Contents

Acknowledgements

All the pictures in this book are from the collections of Bromley Libraries housed in the local studies department of the Central Library and Beckenham Library, except for pp. 118 (top), 121 (bottom) and 127 (both), which are included by kind permission of Joyce Walker.

The following pictures are from the Geoffrey Tookey collection at Bromley Libraries and are included by permission of R.S. Tookey: pp. 12 (top), 18 (top), 24 (bottom), 44 (bottom), 45 (top), 58 (bottom), 60 (bottom), 61 (bottom), 75 (both), 76 (both), 85 (top), 93 (bottom), 96 (bottom) and 102 (bottom).

Pictures on pp. 23 (top), 26 (both), 28 (bottom), 30 (bottom), 39 (bottom), 51 (bottom), 52 (bottom), 53 (top), 55 (top), 82 (both), 88 (bottom), 90 (top), 98 (both), 104 (top), 105 (top), 106 (bottom) and 108 (both) are from the Copeland collection at Bromley Libraries and are included by permission of A.C. Johns.

Pictures on pp. 4, 13 (bottom), 19 (top), 27 (top), 28 (top), 29 (both), 36 (bottom), 38 (both), 40 (top), 42 (bottom), 43 (top), 44 (top), 47 (both), 48 (bottom), 81 (bottom), 83 (bottom), 88 (top), 89 (bottom), 92 (top), 99 (both), 100 (bottom) and 101 (top) are from the Edward Southey collection at Bromley Libraries; those on pp. 22 (bottom), 39 (top), 55 (bottom), 58 (top), 71 (bottom), 74 (bottom) and 89 (top) are from the Francis Frith collection at Bromley Libraries. The top picture on p. 24 is included by permission of E.M. Bacon and the bottom picture on p. 65 is by permission of the Kent Fire Brigade Museum.

I would also like to thank Joyce Walker and Patricia Knowlden for their help with the West Wickham section, David Johnson and Eric Inman for their advice, comments and help with photograph identification, and most of all my colleagues in the local studies department: Elizabeth Silverthorne for her advice on writing style and for proof-reading the text; Loraine Budge for bringing many of the photographs to my attention; Zoë Wetherell for all her researches, both in the library and on the bus, and her help with the introduction and section headers; and Sally Deves and David Gavan for 'holding the fort' while I was busy with the book. It could never have been completed without them.

Introduction

It was the administrative changes of the 1930s that brought Beckenham and West Wickham together; until then they had been neighbours but very much separate communities. Beckenham's history dates back to at least 1086, when it appears in the *Domesday Book*, referred to as 'Bacheham'. This probably means 'Beohha's village' in Anglo-Saxon. Who Beohha was is not known; he may have been an early Saxon settler or landowner. An alternative meaning is the village on the (river) Beck, but this is now thought to be less likely, the river having been named from the village.

There has been settlement in the area since the Iron Age; remains from this period have been found in Toots Wood, Shortlands. Roman pottery has also been found, but there are no signs of major settlement during this period. The London to Lewes Roman road passed close to the centre of both villages. Entering Beckenham near the present site of Greycot Road, it headed south, crossing Bromley Road near to the site of the Theatre Centre. It then ran to the west of Wickham Road and passed behind the Chinese (Park Langley) Garage, through the Langley Court estate and into West Wickham. Crossing the north end of Hawes Lane, Glebe Way near Ash Grove and Corkscrew Hill it then passed to the west of the church. Further south, the present Kent-Surrey border follows the route.

The centre of Beckenham seems to have remained in the same place since medieval times. There is no mention of a church in the Domesday survey but listing churches was not its purpose so there may have been one even before then. A church of some kind probably existed by 1070 and by 1120 there is definite evidence of its existence. Rebuilt about 1340 and again between 1885 and 1902, St George's church remains today. Opposite was the Manor House, also of medieval origin. Occupied by the lord of the manor, it was from here that the village was run. The old village stretched from the west end of the present High Street to Chancery Lane in the east. Beyond this was farmland attached to Kent House, Eden and other farms, the old estates of Kelsey and Langley and the ancient manor of Foxgrove.

As with many places near London, the arrival of the railway in 1857 was the catalyst for change. In the next few years villa-style housing began to develop: at first around Beckenham station, soon to become Beckenham Junction, but soon further away as the Cator family, major landowners in Beckenham since the eighteenth century, realized the potential of new housing and leased much of their land for development. At first they insisted on large houses only, set in half an acre of land, in order to ensure that the influx of new residents was restricted to the wealthier classes, but gradually they became more flexible as the market for larger houses became saturated. Smaller housing came to dominate the Clock House area, much of it built by Francis Ravenscroft of the Birkbeck Building Society.

Following the First World War, the town, as it had by now become, grew further still with Shortlands, Park Langley and the Kent House area undergoing development. Beckenham was now in reality a suburb of London, although it officially remained a large Kentish town with aspirations to become a borough like neighbouring Bromley and Lewisham.

In 1935 Beckenham's application to become a borough was successful but only on condition that West Wickham be included too. Until then it had been part of Bromley Rural District administered from Orpington.

West Wickham developed much later than its northern neighbour but its history is just as ancient. Wickham is a name of Roman origin, indicating a Romano-British settlement which was later taken over by Saxons. As in Beckenham, Roman remains have been found, close to the line of the Roman road.

Early settlement seems to have been more scattered than in Beckenham. The oldest was probably around St John's church; only later did the present centre, around the High Street, originally known as Wickham Street, come to dominate.

The arrival of the railway in 1882 made surprisingly little difference to the village, the population rising only from 1,262 to 1,301 between 1891 and 1921. From the mid-twenties, however, there was rapid development and within ten years the character of the whole place had changed. West Wickham, like Beckenham before it, had become a London suburb; the removal of the old stocks tree from the High Street signalled the end of the old village.

The photographs in this book, taken mainly from the substantial collections at Bromley Central and Beckenham Libraries, follow a route from the north-west corner of Beckenham via the town centre, Shortlands and Elmers End to finish in West Wickham. They date mainly from the nineteenth century and chronicle the change from village to borough. Many of the scenes are unrecognizable today, but a few are surprisingly unaltered.

Organ grinder and monkeys, St George's Road, Beckenham, c. 1900.

One

Lawrie Park
and Clock House

Beckenham is saucepan-shaped. To the north west of the main part of the town is a narrow strip running between Sydenham to the north and Penge to the south, as far as the junction at the north end of Crystal Palace Parade. Although usually referred to as part of Penge or Sydenham, it is historically and administratively part of Beckenham. Robert Borrowman in his Beckenham Past and Present, published in 1910, explains its existence as follows.

'There is a tradition that centuries ago an unknown corpse was found on the top of the hill where the Crystal Palace now stands and that as the authorities of the parish in which it was found declined to bury it, those in Beckenham did so, and removed the body, claiming in return the land on either side of the body and a strip back to the original boundary of Beckenham parish.'

Modern historians prefer the more prosaic explanation that it relates to the irregularly shaped boundaries of the lands of Kent House Farm. The area of the 'pan handle' is now part of the Lawrie Park estate, named after the developer who bought land from the Crystal Palace Company and began to build houses there in the 1870s.

The remainder of the area to the west of the High Street is generally known as Kent House, to the north, and Clock House, the southern part. These names derive unsurprisingly from two old houses whose lands took up a substantial part of this area. Until the developments of the 1880s, much of this area was farmland interspersed with smaller farms and cottages.

Looking north west along Crystal Palace Park Road at its junction with Sydenham Avenue. Prior to the re-erection of the Crystal Palace in Penge in 1854 the main road from Penge to Dulwich followed a more southerly route through what is now the park from the Penge gate at the end of the High Street. It rejoined the present route at the north end of Crystal Palace Parade. When the park was laid out, a new northerly route was chosen around the perimeter named Crystal Palace Park Road. Lined with large villas, it looks quite mature in this view from the turn of the twentieth century. Sydenham Avenue was part of the Lawrie Park estate. Much of this area was redeveloped after the war to allow for the building of the LCC Chulsa estate (named after a nearby large Victorian house which straddled the Beckenham-Sydenham boundary). This corner survived longer, however, and has recently been redeveloped with town houses.

Alexandra School was on the north side of Parish Lane and opened around 1879. Originally an elementary school taking children up to the age of twelve, it eventually closed in 1968 when it was a boys' secondary school. The pupils transferred to the new Kelsey Park boys' school in Manor Way. Pictured here are two classes from 1917. Above is a pillow-lace class, a treat on Friday afternoons; Agnes Paton, the head teacher, is pictured in the back row. Below is a flower dance display, performed in crêpe dresses at Christmas, with each dancer representing a different flower for each month. Flats now occupy the site.

Kent House, 1951. The house is so named because it is the first house in Kent as you come from Surrey. Its history has been traced back to 1240 when it was owned by St Catherine's Hospital. Originally a farmhouse, it often had strong connections with the City of London. In the seventeenth century it was occupied by the Lethieulliers, descendants of Sir John Le Thieuller, Sheriff of London. Later, in 1784, John Julius Angerstein, a member of Lloyd's of London, became the owner. William Makepeace Thackeray, author of *Vanity Fair*, stayed here, as did Samuel Pepys the diarist. In the closing years of the nineteenth century it was a nursing home and later a hotel. Research during the 1950s uncovered the building's great antiquity but this was insufficient to prevent its demolition in 1957 to be replaced by a block of flats.

Penge (now Beckenham) Road, looking west from the corner of Barnmead Road, *c.* 1885. The houses on the right are little altered but the other side was still being developed at this date. The Congregational chapel was short lived; built around 1880, it was gone ten years later, by which time the new Congregational church in Crescent Road was open. See also p. 89.

THE PROMENADE BECKENHAM

Looking the other way, Beckenham Road has a more finished look in around 1910. The two shops on the right are the same as those next to the chapel in the above picture and survive today.

The Clock House area was developed with small houses, in contrast to the Cator Estate lands to the north. The small gardens of the area were supplemented with open spaces and allotments. Here in a 1920s view from the railway behind Churchfields Road, the Crystal Palace can be seen on the horizon.

The Orthodox Anglican church of St Michael and All Angels began life in 1877 in Harding's Lane, but on the opening of Holy Trinity in Lennard Road, it moved to Birkbeck Road where in 1899 a permanent building was started. It is shown here in 1906, the year it opened, still under construction. Building continued until 1935 but on 25 March 1944 it was destroyed by fire in the last manned wartime air raid on the town. It was rebuilt facing Ravenscroft Road and reopened in 1956.

St Augustine's church in Churchfields Road was begun in 1886. A new hall, pictured above, was started in 1910. Below is a portrait of the clergy and choir of unknown date. A brick church replaced this one in the 1930s; more recently the parish has been united with St Michael's and St Augustine's church has been converted into flats.

Beckenham Road, looking west from Sidney Road, 25 April 1903. Only the gabled building on the far right remains on this side of the bridge. The rest were destroyed on 2 August 1944 when a V1 flying bomb made a direct hit on Mrs Richards' dining rooms towards the far end of the parade on the left side. It fell during the lunch hour and forty-four people were killed. The Clock House pub now stands on the point of impact. After the war the road was widened, completely changing the character of the area.

Looking the other way from almost the same spot towards Clock House station, this view from just after the end of the Second World War shows the damaged but repairable shops adjoining the station with Clock House Parade in the background. This view is little changed today.

Clock House station, 1903. The New Beckenham to Addiscombe line opened in 1864 but there was no station where it passed under Beckenham Road until 1890. Named after the large house opposite, the station is seen here virtually as constructed. To the right is the garden of Sidney Lodge. The pillar box was later to be moved to the far end of Clock House Parade.

Clock House Parade, looking towards the station, c. 1910. Built around 1906, the parade has been threatened with redevelopment several times. Even so, it survives substantially unaltered.

Clock House under snow, c. 1893. There has been a substantial house on this site since at least 1623; this building, on the left with the chimneys, dated from around 1713. It is so named because of a large clock on the roof of the stables (see below). The house was demolished in 1896 to be replaced by the Technical Institute and public baths, now The Studio and Leisure Centre. The clock was transferred to Beckenham Place Park. On the right is Elm Road Baptist church (see p. 22) and in the foreground is the undeveloped site of Clock House Parade.

After demolition, part of the stables remained and were taken over by Eldridge and Sons, jobmasters. A jobmaster was a man who kept livery stables and let out horses and carriages for a specific job or period.

The area opposite Clock House station remained undeveloped long after the rest of the area was built up. Part became a nursery but the rest was undisturbed until 1926. Here, the last original tree on the Clock House estate is being removed to allow for the shops pictured at the bottom of page 16 to be built.

The public baths were opened in 1902 and are seen here as they originally appeared. The pool could be boarded over when required to allow for conversion into a meeting hall. Substantially altered in the thirties, the baths survived until 1996 when they were deemed beyond repair and demolished. A new swimming complex is now under construction.

Clock House Road, Beckenham.

Jillard's Photo Series. 9385.

Clock House Road is one of the roads of smaller houses developed south of Beckenham Road in the 1890s. It was the childhood home of Enid Blyton for several years. Only the road humps and permanent lines of parked cars alter the view today.

Beckenham was very late to acquire a public library. Bromley, Lewisham, Croydon and Penge all had libraries by the end of the nineteenth century, but continual opposition from the older inhabitants who saw a library as part of the creeping suburbanization of the town meant that it was March 1939 before the new central library pictured here was finally opened. The gates and railings were gone within a year, sacrificed for the war effort. The front yard is now grassed over but the building is little changed externally apart from the main entrance, which was moved to the side about ten years ago.

The junior department of the library in 1939. The stage designed for library events was removed in 1987, as were many of the oak shelves.

When the First World War broke out Beckenham was building a number of new schools. One of these was Balgowan. Named after a town near Pietermaritzburg in South Africa which featured prominently in the Boer War, it was completed in 1915 and was immediately turned into a military hospital as pictured here. After the war, as Balgowan Central School, it took boys and girls from five to fourteen. Today it is a primary school.

Designed by Edward Mountford, later architect of the Old Bailey, Elm Road Baptist church opened in 1883 before the development of the surrounding streets. The early date of the photograph is shown by the newly planted trees in Elm Road.

Before the development south of Beckenham Road, the area between High Street and Queen's Road was part of the Beckenham Lodge estate. The Steward's House pictured here in around 1875 was on the corner of what is now Elm Road, opposite the church. The change that occurred in less than ten years is difficult to believe.

Beckenham Road at the junction with Hayne Road, 24 April 1903. This is another view showing the affluent nature of this part of Beckenham. Haddon, the large house on the right, has been replaced by flats and the formality of the walls and hedges has been eroded, but much remains.

Woodbrook was a private school in Hayne Road run by Miss G. Mead. She appears in this school group from 1935, seventh from the right in the second row.

Beckenham Lodge from the rear, shortly before demolition, *c.* 1884. The age of the building is unknown, but it was certainly built before 1797. Its front was on Croydon Road. It was for many years the home of the Banyer family. By the time of the demolition, the estate had shrunk considerably. In the foreground are the gardens of the newly erected houses in Hayne Road; Westfield Road and Barclays Bank now occupy the site.

Two

High Street

The High Street has always been the centre of Beckenham life; with its distinctive double bend it has followed the same route throughout history. Early photographs show a typical Kentish village street such as can still be found in rural parts of the county. Small shops, cottages and workshops abound, interspersed with long-established pubs and occasional larger houses such as Village Place and the Manor House.

The arrival of the railway in 1857 brought rapid urban development to the top end of the town, so by 1900 the area around the station and the rebuilt church was densely built up. The lower end of the High Street remained primarily rural in appearance until after the First World War. By 1939 the general look of the present-day High Street was established.

Since 1945, development has been piecemeal. New Safeway, Sainsbury and Waitrose supermarkets have been established as has a neighbourhood Marks and Spencer. A few offices have replaced smaller buildings but the traditional individual shops still predominate. The recent appointment of a town centre manager is part of an attempt to ensure the High Street survives and thrives into the new century.

Two views of the junction of Croydon Road and High Street. The picture above dates from 1873 and is looking towards the junction. On the right are buildings belonging to Kelsey Park Farm while ahead is the future site of the war memorial, Regal cinema and Rectory Road. Below is a view from around 1920. The main parade on the left remains. The precursor of Deen's garage, one of the town's longest established businesses, is identified by the petrol pump just behind the signpost. The large tree on the right is all that remained of the Beckenham Lodge estate. On the far right is a sign advertising a film showing at the King's Hall cinema in Penge.

Croydon Rd Beckenham

Site of the Regal cinema, *c.* 1929. Before the cinema was built the site was in regular use as a fairground. On the left, behind the fence, houses are under construction in The Drive.

The Regal cinema, *c.* 1934. It was opened in 1930, became the ABC in 1962 and was tripled in 1979. The organ was American, having been previously installed at a theatre in Pennsylvania, and survived until 1965 when it was removed to Oxfordshire. In 1977 it was bought by an enthusiast, who installed it in his house in Nottinghamshire. The building has recently been listed but is currently under threat of demolition.

The forge in the High Street was situated in the courtyard next to the Bricklayers Arms.

The lower High Street, *c*. 1920. The war memorial has not yet been erected. Although the Beckenham Lodge estate is by now developed and the house demolished, the corner site itself is still covered with trees.

Two views of celebrations in Burrell Row. Originally one of Beckenham's most picturesque roads, it was named after the Burrell family, long time owners of the Kelsey and Langley estates, and led off the south side of the lower High Street. It was developed around 1870 but its character changed completely in the early sixties when the cottages were replaced by two office blocks. The upper view is of celebrations for Edward VII's coronation in 1902, looking towards the High Street. Below, George V's coronation is being celebrated in 1911, this time looking the other way.

Lower High Street looking east, *c.* 1901. Burrell Row is off to the right. The Rolls restaurant building survives, but otherwise the area has been completely redeveloped in the last hundred years. The billboards next to the pram on the right are advertising events at the Crystal Palace.

Lower High Street, *c.* 1863. This very early view is taken from the end of the future Burrell Row and shows a rural village scene. Only Austin's shop (see p. 37) in the middle distance is common to both this and the picture above.

Village Way, c. 1919. Probably named after Village Place, the large building on the left (see p. 32), the street dates mostly from the 1930s, but this small section began earlier. The wooden building on the right was short lived. Built about 1914, it was a terrace of small houses but disappeared when the main part of the road was built. The gable of the Three Tuns, now the Rat and Parrot, at the top right, is the only survival.

The Pavilion cinema was on the other corner of Village Way. Pictured in the year it opened, 1914, and always showing silent films, the Pavilion could not compete with the Regal after 1930 and closed soon after. It was later replaced by shops. Most of the advertisements further down the street are for cars.

Village Place, *c.* 1915. A house was on this site from at least the seventeenth century but the one pictured here was built in 1717 by William Davis. The property first of the Lea family and then the Wilsons, who intermarried, it was at one time known as The Cedars. Used by the military during the First World War, it was demolished in around 1920. The Drive was the original driveway for Village Place.

Cornelius Lea Wilson, owner of Village Place and village squire. He was born in Islington in 1815 but was educated in Beckenham. His father was Lord Mayor of London in 1838. Cornelius' death in 1911 was closely followed by the break up of the estate.

Mary Ann Wilson, wife of Cornelius, in an undated studio portrait. They were married for more than sixty years.

A corner of Village Place gardens in 1908. Their most famous feature was a huge 100ft high elm tree which had steps and platforms built into it, giving spectacular views of the surrounding countryside. Damaged in a storm in 1836, it subsequently disappeared.

The site of Village Place after demolition, *c.* 1926. Compare the view on p. 31. Cedars Parade was built along this stretch of the High Street. This development and that of the Rectory site a few years later were significant in Beckenham's successful application to become a borough in 1935.

The gates of Village Place and the lower High Street in 1926. The boards are advertising the sale of the estate. At the far end of the High Street, the War Memorial, unveiled in July 1921, is now visible. Compare the view on p. 28.

A view from the site of Village Place, impossible to take since Cedars Parade was built. Most of the buildings survive. What is now the Midland Bank is on the left and Pizza Hut is in the centre. The small building on the right has been replaced by a car park.

Village Place gates from the inside. The last cedar after which the estate was originally named is about to be torn down. The Pavilion cinema is visible at the back.

Cedars Parade, *c.* 1929. Ardec menswear shop survives, unchanged in the last seventy years. At this time the Pavilion cinema was coming to the end of its short life.

'THREE TUNS' & AUSTIN'S DAIRY, BECKENHAM, c.1880

The Three Tuns and Austin's shop, *c.* 1880. The Three Tuns, the George and the Jolly Woodman in Chancery Lane are three very old pubs, possibly dating from the seventeenth century. This building was replaced around a century ago by the present mock Tudor one, which was renamed the Rat and Parrot in 1995.

36

Austin's shop, c. 1950. Built in the seventeenth century as a cottage for the Village Place gardener, by 1850 it was a butcher's shop. It remained in this role for over 100 years until it was demolished in 1959 due to woodworm damage. Note Cedars Parade in the background.

The old fire station on the corner of Kelsey Square, c. 1890. In 1872 it was the home of the Rural Sanitary Authority. The fire engine was kept in a garage underneath. On the roof was the fire bell. When the fire station moved to Bromley Road, next to the Public Hall, the bell was used to warn that it was closing time in Kelsey Park. Later on the building was a branch of the YMCA, a greengrocer's and is now a barber's. On the left is Norton the gasfitters while on the right is Ebbs, a dairyman. That building was later demolished and is now the site of the Rat and Parrot car park.

High Street, c. 1925. Smith and Owen were paint merchants and Brawn was a bootmaker; in between was Goddard the fruiterer. Note the George Inn sign on the left.

High Street and Fairfield Road, Beckenham, looking towards the High Street in 1932. Ahead are Adam Bros (drapers), Brigden (corn merchants) and Aylward Bros (ironmongers). By this date they were owned by Weeks and Co. of Bromley.

Christ Church, Fairfield Road. Opened on this site in 1876, the church began in The Avenue in 1873 as an iron church. Christ Church has always been a 'low' church in contrast to the traditionally 'high' St George's. This early picture dates from before the building of the shops next to the George and the church halls in around 1891. The church was badly damaged by a V1 flying bomb on 5 January 1945 but was afterwards completely rebuilt.

Christ Church over sixties' club, probably in the 1930s.

Bowood House, *c.* 1900. Next door to the church halls, which were built at the same time, it was originally the home of a stonemason, and later of a piano teacher. A garage now occupies the site.

Part of Old Village, Beckenham

High Street *c.* 1906. The Old Wood House may have been a medieval yeoman's house. At this date it was divided into three, the main part being 'Ye Olde Curio Shoppe'. It was demolished around 1912 and replaced first by Sainsburys and later by W.H. Smith. To the left is the Adam brothers' drapers shop, while just visible on the right is the Manor House. Note the glass veranda leading from the street to the front door.

A rear view of the Manor House, undated but probably *c.* 1920. Easily confused with the Old Manor House in Bromley Road, this house was next to The Old Wood House in the High Street. Its history is rather a mystery: it probably dated from the eighteenth century but was subsequently added to. It was the home of Dr Percy Curtis for many years. It ended its days as the Royal British Legion before being replaced by shops in around 1932.

Manor House gardens, *c.* 1920. The River Beck ran through the grounds, which were sandwiched between Village Place and the Rectory. The channel shown here with its wooden footbridge led off the river to a large lake where The Drive now is.

Manor House gardens, 1878. The River Beck has always been prone to flood. On 11 April 1878 a wall beside the grounds of the Old Manor House which had been holding back flood water collapsed, flooding the High Street as far as the Manor House. In an attempt to prevent a repeat the river was culverted where it crosses the High Street. This was only partially successful.

Leach's cottages, c. 1870. This was one of a number of small alleys leading off the High Street in the nineteenth century, just west of the Manor House. It disappeared at about the same time as the Manor House, around 1932.

High Street, *c.* 1951. The George Inn on the right is another of Beckenham's ancient pubs. It has never been completely rebuilt but has rather evolved; it dates from at least 1662 when it appears in hearth tax records. It was the starting point for the London stagecoach in the eighteenth century.

T.S. Ayling, *c.* 1900. Established in Bromley in around 1790, this local family opened a branch in Beckenham in 1899. A second branch existed at no. 50 for some years. They later moved to no. 224 and were still trading in the town in the 1990s.

The High Street at the junction with Burnhill Road, 1927. On the right are council offices, soon to move to the new town hall which opened in 1932, and the International Stores. In the centre is the old parish clerk's house, about to be demolished for road widening. By this time it was a laundry.

The Forge, Burnhill Road, *c.* 1900. Compare this with the forge on p. 28.

The Greyhound Hotel, *c.* 1870. This old building dated from before 1691, although it obtained a drinks licence only shortly before this picture was taken. For much of the nineteenth century it was the home and surgery of Dr Stilwell. Altered many times, it was completely rebuilt in 1962 with an office block above, since renamed Flat Foot Sam's.

Beckenham High Street, looking east in 1903. This was the commercial heart of Beckenham a century ago and has changed little since.

Thornton's Corner, looking west, *c.* 1890. T.W. Thornton, after whom the corner is named, was a printer and stationer originally from Norwood. Established in business on this site by 1879, he bought the fledgling *Beckenham Journal*, then a monthly paper, and converted it to a weekly. It remained the best selling paper in Beckenham throughout its life. Thornton's continued to produce the paper until the mid 1950s from a press in Kelsey Park Road until it was sold to the *Kentish Times* group, who retained the original name until 1985. They also produced Beckenham's first street directory from 1885 and for many years ran a commercial lending library. In later life Tom Thornton, who lived until 1933, moved to Kelsey Square and became an important figure in the town. Thornton's survives as a name in the High Street, still selling cards and stationery, but the business is no longer in the family.

Manor Road at the corner of Kelsey Park Road, *c.* 1900. A further flood at this corner shows that the culverting of the river Beck at this point after the 1878 floods was not a complete success (see p. 42). (see p. 42)

More floods at the same spot, 15 September 1968. A Green Line RF class coach struggles through the water on a Gravesend-Windsor service on route 725. The building behind, damaged during the war, was rebuilt in 1989 as an estate agency.

Thornton's Corner in around 1920, looking towards the future site of the telephone exchange on the corner of Kelsey Park Road. Note the open-top bus on the left. Ahead, the hoarding behind the street sign is advertising a film at the King's Hall cinema in Penge.

Church Hill, *c.* 1880. The trees on the right mark the boundary of the Old Manor House estate. The medieval parish church, pulled down in 1885, is at the top of the hill.

Church Hill, *c.* 1910. The same view as above, thirty years later. The police station (built in 1884) and the shops on the right remain today, as does the new church tower, completed in 1902.

Beckenham Rectory: an undated view possibly from around 1910, looking east towards the High Street. Beckenham has had a rector since at least the fourteenth century. Until 1773 he was an appointee of the lord of the manor and probably lived on the (old) manor house estate. In that year John Cator bought the manor but did not acquire the right to appoint the rector, so when William Rose was appointed in 1778 he had nowhere to live. As a result this splendid building was erected in the following year, designed by Robert Adam and containing a number of his fireplaces. It was not always the home of the rector and in the late nineteenth century it was a school for a while. The site is now Marks and Spencer's car park.

Beckenham Rectory porch, 1924. After the First World War, pressure on land in the town centre grew. The demolition of Village Place began the process (see p. 40) and the Rectory estate soon followed. By 1924 building had already begun.

Revd Frederick Chalmers (1804-1885), rector of Beckenham from 1850 to 1873. Born in Canada, in his early life he was an army officer but following the death of his wife in 1843 he was ordained. On his arrival in Beckenham he appointed his father-in-law Dr Marsh as curate. His sister-in-law Catherine arrived at the same time.

The Chalmers family and Catherine Marsh, *c.* 1865. Catherine Marsh became interested in the spiritual well-being of the navvies working at the Crystal Palace and the new railways in the 1850s, even holding garden parties for them at the Rectory. She was also the author of several books.

Beckenham Rectory, 1927. The estate was covered with houses by the time the rectory was finally demolished. This view is from Church Avenue with the houses of The Crescent in the background. The Town Hall was built here in 1932, the Adam fireplaces being transferred to the new building. This in turn was knocked down and replaced by Marks and Spencer, which opened in November 1992.

Rectory Paddock, *c.* 1925. It appears to be full of chimney pots for the new houses in The Drive and Church Avenue. The Paddock bordered the High Street, opposite the church.

Beckenham tradesmen on the move near Beckenham Junction station, *c.* 1870.

Beckenham Junction station, *c.* 1865. The first station in Beckenham, it opened in 1857. It was originally the terminus of a line from Lewisham, but within a year a new line from Crystal Palace to Shortlands made it a through route. This view, looking towards Shortlands, shows the original structure with an overall roof.

Beckenham Junction, 1870. The station is beginning to take on its present appearance. Note the houses in Copers Cope Road on the left.

Beckenham Junction, c. 1925. A more urban view from the same viewpoint as on p. 53. The buildings on the right were casualties of the war.

Railway Hotel, High Street, c. 1905. The hotel was built in the same year as the station, 1857. The West Kent Hunt met here until 1905 when they disbanded due to a lack of suitable land to hunt over.

The last horse bus leaves Beckenham Junction for Penge shortly before the First World War.

High Street, from the corner of Bromley Road, *c.* 1955. The large building with the pillars is the electricity showrooms dating from the 1930s and originally run by the town council. They were later taken over by the London Electricity Board. Behind is St George's church house, built around 1893 and used mainly as a meeting hall. It survived until 1960 when a new hall replaced it in Albemarle Road. The old site was developed as more shops.

High Street, Beckenham, from Southend Road, *c.* 1910. All the buildings on the left were destroyed in the V1 attacks in July 1944. An office block replaced the nearest building. The rest became the open space known as Beckenham Green.

One of a series of views taken from the top of St George's church tower on its completion in 1902. The parade in the centre, built in 1885, survives, as do the single-storey buildings adjacent to the station. In the distance the large houses of the Cator estates are visible through the trees.

Bromley Road, *c.* 1885. This is the historic heart of Beckenham: the Old Manor House (centre) was the centre of administration from medieval times. In 1882 it became the offices of the Beckenham Local Board. At the same time the stables (left) became the fire station, moving from Kelsey Square (see p. 37). Part of the old manor was demolished to be replaced with the distinctive Public Hall (centre left). At the same time, the London and County bank (right), now the NatWest, appeared. Although the Old Manor House has been rebuilt as an office block behind the façade, the view is remarkably similar today.

Public Hall, c. 1910. A close up showing the ornate veranda which was added around 1900 but removed around 1950. The poster to the right of the door is advertising Beckenham Tennis Week. On the right is the side entrance leading to the premises of 'The Club', established in 1884 and still going strong.

Another view from the church tower in 1902, this time looking south east. The Public Hall and fire station are in the foreground. To the left is Bevington Road Methodist church (built 1887), which has lost its spire in recent years. Manor Road and Bevington Road run in the centre ground, while at the back Court Downs Road is being built up. The Court Downs houses have been mainly replaced with flats in the last thirty years.

The lich-gate of St George's church, before 1867. Described in 1906 as 'one of the oldest and most perfect in the county', it was the only feature of the medieval church to survive the building work of the 1880s unaltered. It is claimed that in the early nineteenth century watchers used to lie in wait on the roof rafters looking out for 'body snatchers'. Its more usual purpose was to shelter the coffin and mourners at funerals while they waited for admission to the church. It was here that the formal ceremony would begin.

Beckenham church from the direction of Bromley Road School, before the extension of the graveyard in 1865.

Another very early view of the graveyard, this time *c*. 1875. Despite the recent extension it is already looking very cluttered.

The graveyard extension is clearly visible in this photograph, dating from around 1874.

One of the last views of the old church, taken in the year it was pulled down (1885). The new London and County bank is on the right, while behind the fence on the left are the rectory grounds.

Looking towards the east end of the interior of the old church, *c.* 1880. By this time, despite the enlargement of both the graveyard and the building in 1865, the building was far too small for a town with a population of more than 13,000; therefore the decision was taken to rebuild it entirely. The rebuilding took place between 1885 and 1887.

St George's church after the rebuiding, c. 1890. The work was carried out by Cornish and Gaymer of North Walsham, Norfolk, at a cost of £18,000. Note the incomplete tower with its temporary wooden roof. The bells were housed here until the tower was completed in 1902.

The bells of St George's church, ready for rehanging. Two bells were replaced in 1903, but the others were transferred from the old church and date from between 1624 and 1796.

Dedication of the new church tower in 1902. The procession is about to enter the church.

The new church tower. The bells have been hung but the roof is not yet complete.

This postcard was issued by Holdsworth at Kent House post office as a special Christmas issue in 1904. It may be a genuine photograph of the new church covered in snow or, perhaps more likely, the snow has been drawn on.

A London General bus on route 109 – Penge to Shooters Hill via Chislehurst – outside St George's church in 1925. The 109 was a forerunner of the present day 227.

Beckenham fire brigade hose cart, 1875. Originally used at the fire station in Kelsey Square, it was transferred to the Bromley Road station in 1882.

Beckenham fire brigade in the yard at Bromley Road, c. 1905. The tricycle seems to have been newly delivered.

A dressmaking class for Form 7 at Bromley Road Girls' School, *c.* 1910.

St George's Road, *c.* 1935. St George's Road was a Victorian development which was still looking smart in this pre-Second World War view. Apart from Bromley Road School, the low building at the far end, the whole area was destroyed in the double V1 attack in July 1944. Today Beckenham Green is on the right and there is a car park on the left.

St George's Road from the church tower, 1902. Apart from the graveyard, the whole area was covered with high density housing. In the distance, the larger houses of The Avenue on the far side of the railway are visible. In complete contrast to the view on p. 58, looking the other way, virtually nothing remains today.

Bromley Road Schools, showing the bell turret on the east side of the main building, 1899. The buildings dated from 1818 and underwent an extension in 1858.

Bromley Road Schools, again in 1899. The garden was destroyed in 1906 when the building was further extended.

Bromley Road Schools from St George's Road, in 1899. It is now an infants' school.

Three

Foxgrove and
New Beckenham

There were two ancient manors in Beckenham: Beckenham Manor itself, centred around the parish church, and Foxgrove Manor, to the north east. Dating back to before 1350, Foxgrove eventually became part of the Langley estates in 1765 and in 1793 passed to the Cator family as part of a land swap. New Beckenham was also part of the Cator estates; it principally covered the lands of Copers Cope Farm, north of the rectory and Village Place, and land to the east of Kent House.

When Beckenham Junction station opened in 1857, these two areas, close to the station and owned by the forward-thinking Cators, were ideally placed to be developed for housing. Copers Cope was quickly renamed New Beckenham, the station of that name opening with the line to Addiscombe in 1864, and the fields were quickly filled with housing. The Foxgrove area was not far behind; the farmhouse which had replaced the manor was demolished in 1878. As an early development, the houses were mainly of the larger type and since the war many have been first converted into flats and then later demolished, to allow for purpose-built blocks.

River Ravensbourne, *c.* 1920. The Ravensbourne forms the boundary between Bromley and Beckenham. This view north of Bromley shows the river winding through Beckenham Place Park.

Foxgrove Farm, *c.* 1870. The manor of Foxgrove dates from before 1350 but the original building was demolished around 1830 and no pictures of it are known to survive. This farmhouse built by the Gibbons family replaced it. Almost surrounded by a moat it was pulled down in 1878 and the site was built over. It lay just to the south of Foxgrove Road, near the present-day junction with Foxgrove Avenue.

70

Beckenham fire brigade express, 1876. The moat at Foxgrove proved useful to the fire brigade in its final days, as it provided a ready source of water for fire practices. The Avenue, which runs just to the south, was previously known as Moat Road. For many years, residents on the north side reported that their gardens were prone to flood in wet weather.

Beckenham Cricket Ground, Foxgrove Road, c. 1890. Beckenham Cricket Club was set up by Arthur Whaten of Beckenham Lodge (see p. 24) in 1866 and played from the start at this ground on the edge of Beckenham Place Park. Tennis was also played from 1879 and in 1886 Beckenham Tennis Week was introduced. Today it continues to attract players from all over the world who use it as a warm-up event for Wimbledon.

Copers Cope House, formerly Copers Cope farmhouse. It is believed to be the oldest house in the town. In existence in 1783 but probably older, the name is believed to be a corruption of Cooper's Copse. It was enlarged during the nineteenth century. The farm's land formed part of the Cator lands from an early date and was developed as New Beckenham from the 1860s. This is an undated but comparatively modern view. The house, on the corner of Copers Cope Road, is now completely surrounded by houses and flats.

Abbey School, Southend Road c. 1890. Founded in 1866, this boys' private school moved two years later to this purpose-built building. Designed to look like an ancient abbey, it was built on farmland attached to Copers Cope.

Two further views of Abbey School. Above is a rear view across the playing fields and below, a cricket match is in progress. The school was evacuated to the Sussex coast in 1940 but following a wartime fire which destroyed one of the wings, did not return. The school eventually closed at East Grinstead in 1969. The remaining buildings survived until 1960 when they were demolished and replaced by flats called Abbey Park.

Another private school in New Beckenham, this time for girls, was Minshall House at 3 Park Road. Opening in 1868, it survived until 1965. Here the girls are performing *A Midsummer Night's Dream* in around 1894. Minshall Court flats now occupy the site.

St Paul's church, Brackley Road, *c.* 1890. Beginning as a daughter church of St George's in 1864, the original temporary building was replaced with this one in 1872 when St Paul's became a separate parish. It recently celebrated its 125th anniversary.

A plank bridge over the Pool river, Datchet Road, Bellingham, c. 1911. Although not strictly in Beckenham, being just over the border to the north, this picture is of interest as it shows Geoffrey Tookey, one of Beckenham's most important historians, as a child. He is second from the left, wearing the cap. Many of the pictures in this book are taken from his collection which included both old views and newer ones he took himself.

The original New Beckenham station. Opened in 1864, when the Addiscombe branch line opened off the Lewisham to Beckenham line, it was situated near the present day Bridge Road. After two years, the decision was made to resite it north of the junction of the two lines so trains on the Beckenham line could call too. It remains here today. Remarkably, the old station survived for 130 years after closure, but has recently been demolished.

Former level crossing at Bridge Road, *c.* 1895. Before 14 November 1901, the main way across the railway at New Beckenham was the level crossing at the south end of the station. On this date the three-way bridge at Bridge and Blakeney Roads opened. The houses in the distance on the right are the beginnings of development in Kings Hall and Lennard Roads.

The level crossing at New Beckenham station, looking east towards Park Road before closure on 14 November 1901. Pedestrians can still cross the line here by subway.

Four

Croydon Road and Kelsey Park

Croydon Road is as old as the High Street, providing a link with the Surrey town via Elmers End throughout history. A rural lane until around 1880, it became built up about the same time as the Clock House area. The cottage hospital opened in 1872 and the recreation ground in 1891. Most of the area east of Croydon Road was historically part of the Kelsey estate. Dating back to at least 1408, it passed to the Burrell family in 1688. In 1768 they also acquired Langley. Both estates were sold in 1820 and Kelsey changed hands again in 1835, when it was sold to Peter Hoare, a close relative of the Fleet Street bankers. Still mainly undeveloped into the twentieth century, part of the lands was bought by the council in 1911 and converted into a public park. The rest of the estate was built over between the wars, when Manor Way, Greenways, Forest Ridge and neighbouring roads appeared. Even so, with both the park and recreation ground and the only partially developed Kelsey Lane running through the middle, the area still has a pleasant, open feel today.

HAYES H. CARR W. GOODMAN G. POLLETT C. RIBBLE J.T. TURLE J. CREASE A. THORNTON BRIGHT

T.W. JONES V.B. CHALK REV. T. SISSONS A.J. BAKER T.W. THORNTON EDGECOMBE REV. C. GREEN

The official opening of Croydon Road Recreation Ground, 1891. Most of the town dignitaries of the time are pictured here. They include W. Goodman (head of Alexandra Schools), G. Pollett (head of Bromley Road Schools), J.T. Turle (manager of the Railway Hotel), J. Crease (Alderman of the town, after whom Crease Park in Village Way is named), T.W. Thornton (publisher of the *Beckenham Journal*) and Revd C. Green of St Paul's church, who lived to be over 100.

The bandstand in the recreation ground, shortly after opening. The houses in Croydon Road can be seen in the background.

Ladies' cycle ride at the Beckenham Flower Show, *c*. 1900. The Flower Show was an annual event at the recreation ground.

The bowling green at the recreation ground, *c*. 1910.

A balloon flight from the recreation ground. There were two flights in the early years of the twentieth century, the first on Edward VII's Coronation day in 1902 and the second on 12 July 1905. This image could illustrate either event. On each occasion, postcards were taken up in hot air balloons and 'despatched from the clouds' with a request to post the card to an address previously written on it. These were among Britain's earliest balloon posts, the 1902 one being the earliest of all. Few cards from the events survive today and those that do are very valuable.

Another Edwardian view of the recreation ground, showing the oriental shelter and drinking fountain.

This street party was held for Queen Elizabeth II's Coronation in 1953 in Yewtree Road, just off Croydon Road.

Christ Church mission hall, Croydon Road, *c.* 1910. Built in 1906 next to the hospital, the hall remained in Croydon Road until 1931 when the mission was moved to Eden Park. For a short time it acted as St John's church until a permanent structure was built. It then became a church hall but was eventually destroyed by a V2 bomb on 21 February 1945. A new hall replaced it in 1956.

Kelsey Cottage, Kelsey Lane, *c.* 1920. Originally known at Kelsey Farm and built in 1832, it was only a cottage in comparison with the massive Kelsey Manor next door. Lit by electricity long before this was standard, it was renamed Kelsey House after the demolition of the manor but was demolished itself around 1930. Uplands and Forest Ridge now occupy the site.

The Gazebo. Originally standing in Church Hill, the Gazebo was used as a shelter by people waiting for the arrival of Squire Wilson's stagecoach from London and, later, the horse bus from Lewisham. The picture to the left dates from around 1880. By 1926 it had outlived its usefulness and was bought by Tom Thornton, the proprietor of the *Beckenham Journal*, and re-erected in his garden off Kelsey Square. The lower picture shows it in its new home with Mr Thornton standing outside. It was finally destroyed when the garden was developed for housing as Thornton Dene in around 1966.

Kelsey Manor as Kepplestone Ladies' School, c. 1905. Kelsey was never officially a manor but it was an old established estate. There was a house called Kelsey as early as 1408 but this was demolished at the start of the nineteenth century. It was sited nearer to the High Street than the later building pictured here, which was begun around 1790. After purchase by the Hoare family in 1835 the house was altered and enlarged almost continually until the 1890s when the Hoares moved away. From 1895 it was a convent until 1901 when Kepplestone School arrived; but this too moved to a smaller building in Overbury Avenue by 1910. It was becoming difficult to find a use for such a large ornate building. Part of the grounds was sold off in 1911 when Manor Way began to appear. Taken over by the military in the First World War, the manor was demolished in 1921. Greenways now occupies the site.

An interior view of Kelsey chapel. Built in 1869 adjacent to the manor house, this ornate structure was very much in keeping with the owner's style. Boys from Sandhills School regularly sang in the choir. It disappeared with the manor in 1921.

Skating on Kelsey lake, c. 1902. An artificial creation, formed by damming the River Beck, the lake has been an ornamental feature at Kelsey for many centuries. The warmer winters of recent years make skating much less safe today and it is officially discouraged.

Kelsey lake, *c.* 1920. Kelsey opened as a public park in 1913. This early view with mature trees shows what an ideal site it was. The park retains the same atmosphere today.

Love Lane, *c.* 1890. Running from the fair field, now the site of Christ Church and Safeway car park, to Wickham Road, this picturesque route was closed in 1896 and the hedges were grubbed up. Court Downs Road follows a similar route today.

Five

Shortlands and Langley Park

The area to the south and east of the village centre was originally known as Clay Hill. The name Shortlands comes from Shortlands House, but ultimately is derived from the type of cultivation practised here in medieval times, when the narrow, wooded valleys restricted crop growing to short sections of land.

Shortlands House, centre of the Shortlands estate, was built in around 1702 and was owned by the Burrell family. It was the birthplace of George Grote, the historian, and later the home of Conrad Wilkinson, who claimed to own the skull of Oliver Cromwell. It is now Bishop Challoner School.

Development of the estate began in the 1860s, shortly after the opening of the station on 3 May 1858. By 1900 the areas around the station and the new Westmoreland Road were covered with housing; the area in between soon followed suit. Much of the Westmoreland Road area has been redeveloped with smaller houses and blocks of flats similar to the Foxgrove area, but the higher parts, particularly Shortlands Road and the area around the church, retain many of their original houses. St Mary's church opened on 5 July 1868 but was badly damaged by a flying bomb in July 1944 and had to be rebuilt. It finally reopened in 1955.

Langley Park was, like Kelsey, an old Beckenham estate. The name means 'long pasture' and therefore has the opposite meaning to Shortlands. Close to both water and the old Roman road (see the Introduction), the area was settled from an early date and is mentioned in a thirteenth-century document. Originally little more than a farm, it passed through several ownerships including that of the Style family, who developed it into a country house estate. By a combination of marriage and purchase, by 1789 it had been acquired by the Burrell family who already owned Kelsey. In 1820 Peter Burrell, by now Lord Gwydir, died and his heir having more land than he needed sold his Beckenham estates. Langley was bought by the Goodhart family who had made money in sugar refining and insurance. Following the death of Charles Goodhart in 1903 the estate, now in a bad state, was sold again, this time for building land. Over the next thirty years Park Langley took on the appearance we see today.

Chancery Lane, *c.* 1910. Prior to the growth of Beckenham in the 1850s, Chancery Lane was on the eastern edge of the old village. It dates back at least to the seventeenth century, when it was known as Alley Lane. The current name dates from 1854 when the lands around the old workhouse were being reallocated and the Court of Chancery became involved in the process.

C.A. Hardcastle at 1 Limes Road. This picture is difficult to date as Mr Hardcastle does not appear in the street directories, but the shop was occupied by a bootmaker for many years. It is now a private house. The road was originally planted with lime trees.

Beckenham Congregational church, Crescent Road, *c.* 1890. The first congregational services were held in an iron church at New Beckenham station. This permanent building on the corner of Oakhill Road was begun in 1887 and opened the following year. A lecture hall had opened in Oakhill Road in 1878.

Oakhill Tavern, Bromley Road, *c.* 1904. In existence by 1879, it is named after Oakhill, the historical name for the district.

Oakwood Avenue at the junction with Bromley Road, c. 1920. Originally called Green Lane, the road was named after Oakwood House (see below). The road was an ancient route leading from the village to the open countryside of Shortlands and was developed around 1897. Off to the right was the site of the old village workhouse, used to house those villagers who could not support themselves. Following the opening of Bromley Union workhouse in 1845 it was no longer needed and was demolished in 1858. The car on the right is outside the former home of Dr Alexander Barton (1861-1939), an aeronautical pioneer who flew a clockwork airship inside the public hall on 10 March 1899, one of the first demonstrations of powered flight. He was also a keen motorist and was one of the first people in the town to own a car.

Oakwood, c. 1917. This was originally the site of an eighteenth-century house called Clay Hill, the home of Dr James Scott, the famous Bromley surgeon. On passing to his son-in-law, the old building was demolished and replaced with this one in 1847. As with most of the large houses in Beckenham, it was used by the military during the First World War but was pulled down in 1930. Ashmere Avenue was built on the site. The lodge house still survives.

Clare House school, Oakwood Avenue, c. 1905. Opened in 1896 as a boys' preparatory school, it amalgamated with the Abbey School (see p. 73) in 1940 and closed in 1970. The present day Clare House primary school is on the site.

Members of the Valley Lawn Tennis Club, Shortlands, enjoy a trip out in 1906.

Hop fields, Park Langley, in 1870. The Langley estate was still surrounded by countryside at this date. Hop pickers have been visiting Kent from London since the seventeenth century but the arrival of the railways opened up more possibilities for the less adventurous. By this time Langley was only a short walk from Shortlands, Beckenham Junction or Elmers End stations.

Brabourne Rise under construction, c. 1926. In 1908 H. and G. Taylor of Lewisham bought a sizeable section of the Langley estate and began the construction of Park Langley. The development was a slow business and was interrupted by the First World War; it was far from finished when this shot was taken. Brabourne appears to be a word of Scottish origin meaning the stream on the hillside. It is not too fanciful a name for a road which descends into the valley of the river Beck.

Park Langley Garage, Wickham Road, c. 1935. The garage was built by Taylor's in 1929 at the junction of Wickham Road and Hayes Lane, which was formerly known as Looking Glass Corner. The unusual oriental style may have resulted from a competition going on at the time to find original designs for filling stations. It is generally referred to today as the Chinese Garage and became a Grade II Listed building in May 1994.

Shops in Wickham Road, c. 1935. Adjacent to the Chinese Garage, they date from 1929. They were originally envisaged with a colonnade in front, which never materialized.

Johannisbad in Wickham Road, undergoing demolition in 1959. One of the typical large houses that lined this road, it was built between 1899 and 1902. Occupied by the Beney family until the Second World War, it was later converted into flats. Smaller modern houses were built on the site.

Stone Farm, Wickham Road, c. 1905. Sited at Looking Glass Corner, where the Chinese Garage now is, it was sold in 1820 by the Burrells of Langley and survived until 1928.

George (1852-1902) and Charles (1818-1903) Goodhart of Langley. Charles was the son of Emanuel, who had bought the Langley estates when they were sold by Lord Gwydir in 1820. He is pictured here with his third son, George, a tea merchant. On Charles' death the estate was sold for building land.

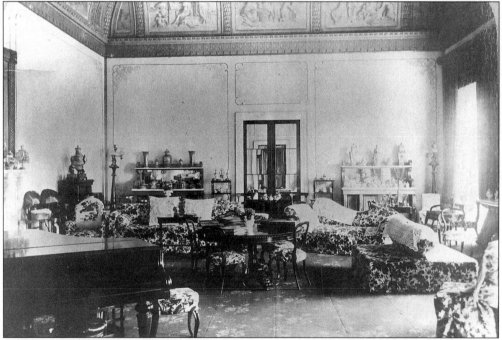

The drawing room at Langley Mansion, c. 1900. Its origins date back to the sixteenth century when John Style began to build a country seat. After the sale of the estate in 1908 it was planned that the mansion would be used as the club house for the new Park Langley golf course. Unfortunately less than three years after opening, it was destroyed in a huge fire on 6 January 1913. Langley Park Girls' School now occupies the site.

Langley Court, c. 1948. This was originally the site of Langley Farm, which was sold in 1885 by the Goodharts and demolished. The new owner, J.L. Bucknall, built this new house designed by local architect James Barnett. Following financial difficulties, apparently resulting from over-indulgence of their favourite hobby, ballooning, the Bucknalls sold the house and grounds to the Wellcome Foundation in 1920. Wellcome established sizeable research laboratories on the site. Following a takeover by Glaxo, the multinational pharmaceutical company, research ceased in 1995 and the site was put up for sale. There are currently plans to return the house to residential use.

Langley Court Cottage, 1949. A survival from the days of Langley Farm, it is sited in the grounds of Glaxo Wellcome. The cottage dates from before 1821, when it is known the clock was repaired. It is sometimes referred to as a chapel but is more likely to have been a farm outbuilding.

Six

Elmers End and Eden Park

Elmers End, at the south western edge of Beckenham, is named after Richard Aylmer, a thirteenth-century landowner in the district. For many years the major building in the area was a moated house, probably similar in style to the original Foxgrove manor house. Situated where South Norwood Country Park now is, the remains survived just long enough to appear on the first edition of the Ordnance Survey map published in the 1860s.

The main population was always around the green where old cottages survived until the First World War although modern development had begun near the station (built in 1864) as early as the 1870s. St James' church and school opened in 1880. By the end of the 1930s, the green was much as we see it today but many of the old buildings on the south side of Upper Elmers End Road survived until the early 1960s.

Eden Park was another of the old estates of Beckenham. Originally known as Eden Farm, by 1807 it was the home of Lord Auckland, formerly William Eden. After 1853 it was no longer lived in and gradually became dilapidated. It had disappeared by 1897, although sometimes it appeared on later maps. The site of the house itself is now occupied by Crease Park, which opened in 1936 in Village Way. The area to the south from here to the station of the same name, which opened in 1882, is usually referred to today as the Eden Park estate. Eden Park was built up between the wars and is similar to the Park Langley estate to the east, except that the houses are more varied in size.

The Odeon cinema at Elmers End undergoing demolition, *c.* 1960. The Odeon was the last cinema to open in Beckenham, on 26 August 1939, when it showed *The Man in the Iron Mask*. Like many late cinemas it had a short life and closed in 1957. Car showrooms replaced it.

Gowland Cottage, Croydon Road, *c.* 1900. This was an old cottage of unknown age, on the corner of Gowland Place, and originally had its own grounds. It survived until 1983, when it was replaced by four modern houses.

The William IV pub, Elmers End, 1900. This is the original building which was of unknown age but possibly dated from the eighteenth century. It was demolished shortly after this and replaced by the present mock Tudor building. The brewers Nalder and Collyers were based in Croydon.

Upper Elmers End Road, 1951. These cottages were soon to be demolished to make way for council flats. They are the same cottages as shown on p. 4.

Number 146 Upper Elmers End Road. This early nineteenth-century building was originally residential, but was used as garage buildings in the 1930s before disappearing during the redevelopment of the area in the 1950s. It was replaced by flats.

Upper Elmers End Road, south of Abbot's Way, c. 1900.

Upper Elmers End Road in 1961, shortly before the arrival of Master's Garage on the right.

UPPER ELMERS END ROAD, BECKENHAM.

Upper Elmers End Road near the present-day entrance to Altyre Way, *c.* 1914.

The Old Brewery, Upper Elmers End Road, *c*. 1938. Dating from before 1880, it was originally the West Kent Brewery. It later became Kempton's bakers, who by the 1930s were specializing in meat pies. As with most of the area, it was replaced with flats in the early fifties.

Oak Lodge, South Eden Park Road, *c*. 1900. Situated on the border of Beckenham and West Wickham, the house dates from around 1820 when Ridle Meadow was bought by William Davis, a grocer from Deptford. It had previously been part of the Langley estates. Originally called Wickham Hatch, the house itself is just inside the parish of West Wickham. For a short time it was the home of E. Fyffe of banana fame. For most of the twentieth century the Schove family lived there. In recent years it has been converted into flats.

Seven

Local People

Many local people are featured throughout the book, as part of the story of the places in which they lived, worked and played. In this section the focus is on those who were known throughout the district. Many of the photographs are from the collection of the late Rob Copeland, who as well as collecting old photographs, made a positive effort to record some of the atmosphere of his own time.

Henry and Eliza Copeland, *c.* 1905. Henry Copeland arrived in Beckenham from Sleaford in Lincolnshire aged twenty in 1862, and began work as a builder. He married Eliza, also from Sleaford, three years later. He founded the firm of H. Copeland, builders and undertakers, in 1874. Originally in the High Street, they moved to their present Bromley Road address in 1885. His grandson, Rob Copeland, was a keen local historian. Many of the images in this book come from his collection.

Ida Watson (1887-1968), *c.* 1905. Author of *The History of West Wickham* (1959), she was the founder of the West Wickham Society and lived in Boleyn Gardens. She was a keen gardener and animal lover. She died in tragic circumstances in November 1968 when her house caught fire.

Beckenham postmen outside the parcel office in Albemarle Road, *c.* 1900.

John Dennis, the last village beadle, *c.* 1900. The village beadle was a church officer whose duties had become obsolete by this date. He succeeded to the office on the death of his father in 1894 and is shown here in the traditional uniform of tasselled hat, gold laced coat and red waistcoat. This must have been a special occasion as his father had been the last to wear the garb while carrying out his duties.

West Wickham volunteer fire brigade outside their headquarters in the High Street, *c.* 1911.

The players of Beckenham Wesleyan Cricket Club, *c.* 1924. The pavilion may be the one at Foxgrove Road.

Victor Thornton in the title role in his production of *Peer Gynt,* in 1928. Son of Tom Thornton, Victor too was involved with the *Beckenham Journal,* being editor for about twenty years after the war as well as producing many local plays and helping to establish the Beckenham Theatre Centre in 1960.

One of the many local characters captured on film by Rob Copeland, the muffin man is seen here in 1929.

Herbert Brown of 43 Chancery Lane, the local chimney sweep. This picture is probably from the thirties but his business dated back to at least 1909.

Eight

Wartime

Beckenham and West Wickham were closely involved in both the First and Second World Wars. The large houses which survived in numbers in 1914 were considered ideal military premises. Not only did they have large grounds for practices and storage of equipment but they were close to London and a short drive from the channel ports from where supplies and troops were sent to the front. Local people too played an active role in the war effort.

In the Second World War, Beckenham suffered mainly from flying bombs. Escaping comparatively lightly from the manned bombing raids of the early war, much of the destruction came in 1944 and 1945, especially from V1s. Eager to avoid destruction in central London, the government put out false information that the early raids were overshooting their targets in the capital. As a result, the Germans put less fuel on board, resulting in them falling short and landing on South East London. Penge was the most bombed town during this period but Beckenham cannot have been far behind.

Beckenham Volunteer Training Corps parade at the Beckenham Cricket Ground one summer during the First World War.

Bomb damage at 58-60 Stone Park Avenue, 20 November 1940. At this time there were raids over London every night.

The 55th Battalion Kent Home Guard, being inspected by George VI at Glebe House, West Wickham in August 1940.

Warden's Post No. 51, Beckenham.

Bomb damage in Albemarle Road, July 1944. Two V1 flying bombs landed in the area during this month. On 2 July one landed on the corner of Albemarle Road and the High Street, destroying the Railway Hotel (see p. 54). Later, on 27 July, St George's Road was the target, the houses in that road being flattened. This is probably a view of the aftermath of the first incident. Apart from the office block opposite the station, most of the area was never rebuilt. The open space known as Beckenham Green was created instead.

A further view on the same morning.

An ambulance on St George's Road, during the Second World War. The mature nature of the trees suggests the picture antedates the devastation of July 1944 but the lack of houses suggests it may have been later.

The end of the war was celebrated with street parties throughout the borough. The picture above shows a party in a garden in Clock House Road on 30 May 1945. Below is a scene from VE Day, 9 May 1945, in Aylesford Avenue off Upper Elmers End Road.

Nine

West Wickham

Prior to 1935, West Wickham had a completely independent history from Beckenham. With its own share of large houses and estates, its history was dominated by the Lennard family, lords of the manor for more than 300 years.

Not all of West Wickham transferred to the new Borough of Beckenham. The rural south around Layham's farm was transferred to Keston, but unlike the rest of that parish which was part of Bromley Municipal Borough, continued to be administered from Orpington until the London Borough of Bromley was set up in 1965.

Post war developments have been limited. From 1956, Glebe Way connected the High Street with Coney Hall, although it was almost forty years before buses acknowledged its existence. The development of Safeway and Sainsbury's supermarkets have changed shopping habits, but less than might be expected. The High Street retains the best selection of small shops in the district. Even the recent introduction of a Red Route throughout its length, where parking and deliveries are banned, has not prevented it continuing to thrive. An affluent little town, West Wickham can face the new century with confidence.

Wickham Hall, High Street. The site was originally part of the Carpenters Farm estate. After Sir Thomas Wilson bought the estate in 1750, he erected a large house, for a while attached to the estates of the Burrells of Kelsey during which time the stables now used by Unigate were begun. Following the break-up of the Burrell lands in around 1820, Wickham Hall passed through several owners, including Revd William Cator, rector of Beckenham, and James Staat Forbes, future chairman of the London, Chatham and Dover Railway. When he left in 1883, it was due to become a convent but instead it was bought by Gustav Mellin. German by birth, he

had made his fortune from baby food. He set about an £80,000 expansion during which materials were imported from all over Europe. The result, illustrated here, shortly after completion in 1897 was likened to Buckingham Palace. Above left is the entrance front, below left, the garden front; above right the view from the summer house and below left from the stables. An interior view can be seen on p.2. Just five years later Mellin died. On his wife's death in 1929 the house was sold and the contents auctioned. The house was demolished in 1931 after a life of less than thirty-five years and houses and shops now occupy the site.

The Alders, *c.* 1910. Situated off the High Street alongside the River Beck, which here follows the old Kent-Surrey boundary, The Alders has a long history. Traditionally lined with cottages since the early nineteenth century, the hedges were, surprisingly considering the name, of hazel. The last two cottages were demolished in 1986. The girl is Rose Acton, who lived in the cottage on the left.

Pond House, High Street, *c.* 1926. Formerly known as the King's Arms and sited at the Croydon end of the High Street, it dated from before 1753. It ceased to be an inn in 1821 when Edward Little renamed it Pond House and converted it into a private house; it remained so for the next hundred years. At the time of this picture it was a solicitor's. It was severely damaged by a flying bomb in 1944 and demolished two years later. Crittenden Lodge and a caravan park now occupy the site.

The White Hart, High Street *c.* 1870. Originally a private house, the White Hart took over the licence of the neighbouring King's Arms in 1821. This building was replaced with the current one in around 1908.

Ribbon Cottage, High Street, *c.* 1860. Outside are members of the Cooper family. Demolished some time before 1931, Curry's is now on the site.

Yates' sweet shop, High Street, c. 1946. The building dates from around 1760 and was originally called Vine Cottage. It was damaged during the war but was restored and is now a barber's shop.

Wickham House seen from the south east in October 1923. A house called Crouches was first built on this site in 1662 but had been renamed Wickham House by 1794. The present building was constructed between 1868 and 1871 to the design of Norman Shaw on the same site as the previous house. In 1881 it was bought by Robert McAndrew, a Liverpool ship owner, whose wife was still in residence in 1923. Sold in 1925, the gardens were built on and the house was converted into shops and flats.

The Swan Inn, *c.* 1890. There has been an inn here since at least 1745, which was called Smethes in 1787, but by 1838 it had acquired its current name. The building illustrated here dates from the 1840s. In front is the ancient Stocks Tree, named for being the traditional site of the village stocks, used for punishing miscreants. Damaged by road widening and drainage works, it was moved to the recreation ground, where it survived until blown down in a gale in 1968. Its remains can be seen at West Wickham Pools.

The Stocks Tree in around 1935, shortly before its removal. The damage to the tree is clear to see. Note the new shops built into Wickham House on the left.

Yew Tree Cottage, opposite the Swan in Station Road, *c.* 1930. The cottage dated from the early eighteenth century and was formerly part of the Ravenswood estate. It was put to a variety of uses and was by this date a tobacconist, with a chimney sweep in the right hand annexe. The cottage was demolished in August 1939 to allow for the building of Glebe Way, but the new road was delayed by the war and did not open until 1956.

A view from an upper floor window of Wickham House, *c.* 1935. The bus on the left is turning out of the High Street. The modern continuation of the High Street, Glebe Way, was built straight through the site of the cottage next to the signpost.

Glebe House, *c.* 1920. This was the original village rectory, built before 1634 and extended in 1712 and 1835. It was sold in 1925 and is now part of a retirement complex.

Ravenswood Hotel, Station Road, *c.* 1925. This was originally the site of Grove House, which dated from before 1660. It was rebuilt in around 1705 and was visited by both Dr Samuel Johnson and William Pitt the Elder, who spent his honeymoon there. In 1842 the Hall family moved in and renamed it Ravenswood. Two of the daughters, Ellen and Emily, kept diaries for most of their lives, extracts of which have been published. Neither married; they remained at Ravenswood until they died, Emily in 1901 and Ellen in 1911. The estate passed to their nephew, who sold it for building in 1922, the house becoming an unsuccessful hotel. The house was sold again and divided, the southern half being replaced in 1932 by the Plaza cinema which itself closed in 1957. Boots is now on the site.

The Dining Room
Wickham College
West Wickham. Kent.

The dining room of Wickham College, Station Road, *c.* 1935. After the division of Ravenswood, the northern half became a private school. It survived until around 1944 when danger from flying bombs caused its closure. The college building was demolished in 1957 and Sainsbury's built a store on the site in 1961.

Wickham Green, *c.* 1870. The Leather Bottle, pictured here, was replaced by the Railway Hotel in 1882. It was on the corner of what is now Station Road, where the lawns in front of the pools are now.

Wickham Green, c. 1937. The old wooden house was Cook's Farm, built in 1484. Shops now occupy the site next to where the station gate once stood.

The first train at West Wickham station, 29 May 1882. Before the 1870s there had already been two proposals to bring a railway to West Wickham, but it was the effort of John Farnaby Lennard of Wickham Court in 1879 that was successful. The line was a branch off the Mid-Kent Railway at Elmers End, which continued as far as Hayes. The locomotive is a Cudworth 0-4-4 back tank.

Red Lodge, The Avenue *c.* 1880. Situated near the present day St Mary's church and originally attached to the Langley estates, it was a farmhouse for most of its life. The upstairs rooms contained sixteenth-century panelling which was transported to the Pennsylvania Museum of Art before demolition of the house in around 1950.

Coney Hall tea gardens, *c.* 1919. Most of the building dates from around 1650, although parts may be medieval; it was refronted in the eighteenth century. Coney Hall was used as St John's rectory from 1925 to around 1975. It is now a private house.

Wickham Court Road, looking north, *c.* 1926. The garage on the right no longer sells fuel. Note the pruned Stocks Tree on the left.

West Wickham National School, *c.* 1900. Opened in 1818, the National School was in School Road, now Wickham Court Road. It was replaced by a new school in Hawes Lane in 1930 and is now Greenhayes private school.

St John the Baptist's church, *c*. 1890. Dating from the fifteenth century, but replacing an earlier building, the church was originally at the heart of village life next to the manor house, as at Beckenham. By Tudor times, however, the focus of village life had moved to the top of Corkscrew Hill, leaving the church and manor isolated on their hill to the south. Even today, the church can be approached across fields.

Wickham Court, *c*. 1900. The ancient manor house was built in around 1475 by Sir Henry Heydon whose family owned it until the end of the sixteenth century when it passed to the Lennard family who held the lordship of the manor into the twentieth century. Sold by the family in 1933, it became first a hotel, then a religious college. Until recently, it was part of the Schiller International University. It is now an annexe to St John Rigby RC School.